The Art of Subtraction

Other Books by Jay Parini

Singing in Time (poems)

Theodore Roethke: An American Romantic (criticism)

The Love Run (novel)

Anthracite Country (poems)

The Patch Boys (novel)

An Invitation to Poetry (textbook)

Town Life (poems)

The Last Station (novel)

Bay of Arrows (novel)

John Steinbeck (biography)

Benjamin's Crossing (novel)

Some Necessary Angels: Essays on Writing and Politics

House of Days (poems)

Robert Frost (biography)

The Apprentice Lover (novel)

One Matchless Time: A Life of William Faulkner

The Art of Teaching (essays)

The Art of Subtraction

New and Selected Poems

by JAY PARINI

GEORGE BRAZILLER, INC.
NEW YORK, NEW YORK

For information, please address the publisher:
George Braziller
171 Madison Avenue
New York, NY 10016

Library of Congress Cataloging-In-Publishing-Data
    Parini, Jay.
    The art of subtraction : new and selected poems /
    by Jay Parini.-- 1st ed.
        p. cm.
    ISBN 0-8076-1546-3 (pbk.: alk. paper)
    ISBN 0-8076-1547-1 (alk. paper)
I. Title.
    PS3566.A65A89 2005
    811'.54--dc22

Design by Jesse Meyers Willenbring
Printed and bound in the United States of America
First Edition

For Devon, who lived as well as read these poems

ACKNOWLEDGMENTS

Thanks to the following magazines,
where many of these poems appeared:
*Agni Review, American Scholar, Atlantic Monthly,
Dark Horse, Georgia Review, Harper's, The Hudson Review,
Iowa Review, Kenyon Review, New Republic, The New Yorker,
Ontario Review, Paris Review, Partisan Review, Poetry,
P.N. Review, Scottish International, Sewanee Review,
Smartish Pace, South Atlantic Quarterly, Tar River Poetry,
Verse, Virginia Quarterly Review,* and *Yale Review.*

TABLE OF CONTENTS

NEW POEMS

AFTER THE TERROR

FISH-EYE VIEW

WHITE CANE

SELECTED POEMS

AFTER THE TERROR

AFTER THE TERROR

Everything has changed, though nothing has.
They've changed the locks on almost every door,
and windows have been bolted just in case.

It's business as usual, someone says.
Is anybody left to mind the store?
Everything has changed, though nothing has.

The same old buildings huddle in the haze,
with faces at the windows, floor by floor,
the windows they have bolted just in case.

No cause for panic, they maintain, because
the streets go places they have been before.
Everything has changed, though nothing has.

We're still a country that is ruled by laws.
The system's working, and it's quite a bore
that windows have been bolted just in case.

Believe in victory and all that jazz.
Believe we're better off, that less is more.
Everything has changed, though nothing has.
The windows have been bolted just in case.

IN TIME OF WAR

We all moved easily within our borders;
you could almost not believe a war
was really going on, though fighters flew
in pairs across the lake and over mountains
and one saw the troops in restaurants
and sometimes in the streets, always polite.

The President assured us all was well.
He had made some eloquent addresses
in the months before the war began.
Now intermittently we heard that victory
was near at hand, that soon the enemy
would fold its tents, pull down its fences.

Children were all taught the patriotic songs.
They sang them in the streets. Employment
in the factories was full, or full enough.
The Boy Scouts marched in serried ranks
in parks, while Girl Scouts baked their cookies
for the young men far away and fighting.

You could still get many distant channels
on the pay TV. A few of them brought
pictures of the war: the refugees who
failed to cross the borders, accidental deaths
in hospitals and streets, the burning tires
and blazing trees and scattering of tribes.

We heard the tallies and assumed the best,
believing in the cycles that must spin,
that war is just a prelude to the peace
that always passes understanding. History
was happy with this pattern, which it knew
by heart, wiping the blood from its big chops.

THE PROPHETS

They come to us from elsewhere,
false and true,
some standing in the park on boxes, shouting,
some on buses, rising
to declare whatever moves them
to their calls for justice, retribution, mercy,
common sense. They bear
a message from the fourth dimension
of their clearest vision,
speaking to an age indifferent to reason.
It is hard to understand their grief,
their anger, and their joy.
A few disciples carry on behind them,
handing out the leaflets,
playing tapes, believing in belief.
Sad, how few words
are true enough to matter,
make us willing to attend a meeting,
answer calls, or rise above the crowd.

THE LOST SOLDIERS

The dead and missing from the foreign wars
come home again.
They've been at sea these many years
in bunks, on deck,
the cobalt waters underneath them, sloshing,
scavenging like gulls in their long wake,
gobbling the body parts,
the bits and pieces cast adrift.
They roam our town in shredded uniforms
and dented helmets,
stand and stare, in parks and public forums,
bleeding from the ears,
the stomach, at the neck,
but now and then
alert enough to raise a wary eyebrow,
wondering what cause
was just enough and equal to the terror
of the little children
who were burned, though probably in error.

STATE OF THE UNION

A cheap motel, the shaggy carpet strewn
with socks, gray hairs, half moons of toenail.
Mold grows slick and green on curtains
in the shower stall. A single cricket
cowers in the drain, too wet to cheep.
The water comes and goes in spurts,
not hot or cold enough to make a difference.
I lay my toweled body on the bed
as dusk turns dark, the traffic slurs.
Outside, blue neon blinks: No Vacancy.
I scratch my belly, stare into the tube.
There is a presidential speech tonight
on every channel. It's about this war
in foreign parts, a little war of choice
designed to keep the world upon a course
that's sane, familiar, and is surely ours.
The Occupation is, of course, expensive.
With a curling lip, he says that thousands
may well die. This will cost real money.
He must ask for sacrifice and patience.
We're privileged to live here, eating chips,
our pitchers overfilled with Coke and beer.
We can't take air-conditioning for granted
or the freedom always to be cool.
In misery, I pounce upon the set.
But even when I turn the TV off
I hear his voice. It drags and drones.
He's probably recording in the room next door.
That flag behind his head is just a prop.
The podium is false, and nobody can see
he hasn't bothered to put on his pants.

OCCUPIED COUNTRY

The bees now, zumming over flowers,
hesitate a moment, then pass on.
The children only dance indoors.

The government believes the worst about us.
They have put up signs:
Your neighbors may have come from somewhere else.

I'm looking over shoulders not my own.
I don't give out my number anymore.
I listen for the feet outside my door.

SLEEPING THROUGH THE STORM

All night the black rain soaked my body.
I could not get up.
The lightning zigzagged through my brain.
I listened at the wall, where voices
indistinctly begged for their brief lives.
I tried to shout, but words like arrows
fell into the grass short of their target.
I could smell the bacon fat downstairs,
the dirty laundry in the wicker basket.
I could hear the little ones upset.
The village idiot was at the door.
The fire department wanted me to dress
and join the company around the fire.
The armies of the night, like frenzied beetles,
marched on cities. Ants assembled
in a long red line, prepared to follow.
I could not get up.

LION'S DEN

This lion's prowling in a den of Daniels.
He was not cut out for such destruction.
It was just another pleasant Sunday
in the well-swept cage.
He swatted flies with his big tail
and yawned and stretched.
But then his breakfast never came.
His lunch went missing.
Now they've pushed him into this arena,
where the meek and mild recite their prayers
and the only roar is from the crowd,
who seem to find the spectacle amusing.
He will use the gifts he has been given—
teeth and paws—
but even as he growls he knows the truth,
that these poor animals won't know
how much he really doesn't even care
for their lean flesh, their soft small bones.

BIG TOP BLUES

The circus has been closed till further notice
as you might have heard.
The tigers have gone home.
The clowns have all been given titles.
Elephants on tip-toe shop for china
for their new apartments in the town.
The monkeys have begun to type their memoirs,
and the lady formerly so fat
won't touch the pie, the cookies, or the cream.
An empty highwire vibrates in the wind,
a soulful whine
like poetry that nobody will hear.
The ticket-takers still accept your money
but the empty rings
refuse to circle in the sawdust dark.

GOD'S PROBLEM

Sunlight is the half of it, *Signore*.
Have you noticed how the waters blacken
and grow cold? How flowers turn away
in protest, closing fists against the night?
It was all beyond mere calculation,
you will say. Your hand was busy elsewhere,
painting daisies in the greenest pastures,
brightening the corners of old parlors
with a golden beam or two of cheer.
You never really understood that we,
not quite so lofty as your highness,
wouldn't hang around, waiting for dawn.
We liked the dark streets of the city,
all the smoky dens, the rolling dice.
A few of us acquired a certain power.
We learned that killing was so easy,
and that those who really did object
could just go lump it. You were busy
elsewhere, finding rhymes for silly words,
devising universal schemes to keep
the physicists all guessing, endlessly
attending weddings, funerals, and births,
where everyone said nice things in your name.
But, dear *Signore*, look around you.
Empty rice bowls, corpses piling up
in vacant cellars, madmen on the loose
in three-piece suits, in armored cars,
with flags and bodyguards to shield their vice.
You surely didn't mean for this to happen,
but, dear God, whatever did you mean?

LISTENING TO THE BBC WORLD SERVICE,
LATE AT NIGHT

My little radio, my shortwave
monster of confession.
Small black box of many sorrows
and a joke or two.
It turns you on to brag about
destruction, tell me that
in jungles heads are rolling,
that the city towers tumble on themselves.
In deserts, things are even worse.
The children, too,
it seems, must suffer
as the world goes boom.
Sometimes I hate what you
have said, can't stop
from saying. I could fling you out
the window testily
in high green grass,
but everybody knows
you'd just keep squawking.
Better let you scream.

AT THE MANNEQUIN CONVENTION

Everyone is here, some dressed to kill,
some showing off their joints and plastic skin.
The hair looks real on those up front,
the politicians, who accept the steady silence
that confronts them as a wry assent.
The delegates have come from far and wide
to show support, to celebrate their tribe,
demand a little more of this or that:
more window dressing, better heat in winter,
air-conditioning throughout the summer months.
Their eyes are pointing in the same direction.
There is no one here with arms akimbo,
though in some back room heads are removed
and placed in boxes and shipped back in shame
to factories in China and Korea.
There was some objection to the way they winked
without a sense of when it was allowed.
One pretty blonde apparently objected
when they stood her up in a bikini.
She just fell apart. They shipped her home
in separate boxes, marked defective.
There is some demand for mannequins of color,
but the shipments stalled; the few who made it
have been put on stage, in listening pose.
The speaker has the blackest hair of all,
the whitest teeth, an ambiance of warmth
but also power. They have wrapped his hands
around the podium. He's so damn real,
the audience keeps saying to themselves.
Rude silence reigns here, ratified, correct.
The guards have plastic bullets in their guns.
The company would rise on all their hinges,
clap and clatter, if they only could.

THE PRESIDENT ALONE

The president sips coffee, all alone
in his white house.
The cameras cannot invade his mind.

He doesn't understand why some won't cheer
when he cries war
against the enemies of right and good.

The bombs must fall. The helicopters must
arrive in clusters and conclude their efforts.
We will show real mercy in the end.

We don't want war, not war exactly,
he explains politely
to the other president who lives inside him.

He adjusts his tie.
We want the terror just to go away.
We are the terror, somebody has said.

How can that be? We're free and easy.
We have walked our little kids to school.
On Sundays, in the park, we toss the balls.

The president admires the silver spoon
beside his cup.
His room is cool and bright and quiet.

He has been elected, after all.
His body is a powerful machine.
His eyes are steady and his hands are clean.

DEMOCRACY

Near dusk, the vote is called.
So one hand rises, then another,
in the pine-planked room of men and women,
as the little children suck their thumbs.

There is broad assent
among the many seated in the pews,
in balconies, on window ledges, standing at the back.

In shadow, there are those who disagree,
who hunch in anger, clutch their elbows,
tip their heads away from what was said.

A few of them will never leave this hall
until the darkness, which has just begun,
grows inside out,
and they walk one by one into the night
with empty pockets, with a granite heart.

IN THE VILLAGE OF THE NEW CENTURY

Crows settle in the fists of trees
along the mud roads into open country.
Huts grow cold as clay.

The children have all lost the pick-up sticks
they used to play with
in the days when firewood
could be found,
when logs came wheeling into town
on wood-frame carts,
when markets overwhelmed
with pomegranates, dates and figs,
with honey in its combs.

Not since the sky fell on their village.

Long, black shadows striped the fields.
Red flowers, detonating heads, unmade their beds.
The rain like blood ran down their cheeks.

Now children graze the dump together
in a newfound freedom.

There are mothers, too, and fathers wandering
like bits of paper in the smoke of wind.

PENELOPE

When nothing in the world seems quite all right,
it takes some patience just to watch and pray.
Think of Penelope, pulling apart by night
the subtle stitches that she wound by day,
believing that Odysseus would find his way
through time and certain turbulence to light
again upon her shore, this time to stay.

FISH-EYE VIEW

FISH-EYE VIEW

Not everyone's so lucky.
Long before the world drew up its shades,
we gathered at the table, trembling,
and drew lots. A friend of mine,
who washed his hands before and after
every single meal, became an earthworm.
One, a teller of white lies,
now swings his guts
in some damp forest, limb to limb,
spinning his web. He's looking for
a fly who was my neighbor
in the mist before: always annoying
with his busy drone in my good ear.
That guy who hit on anything in skirts
is baying at the moon, far from the pack,
lost in the howl of his desire.
One girl who favored woolen sweaters
has become a moth in her own closet.
But I'm sitting pretty in Des Moines,
in this bright mall, one of a tank
of ritzy goldfish. Not so bad,
with easy money all around me,
and a gilded life for me to spend.

PEACHES

With a ladder strung for me to climb,
the long branch quivering,
I rise toward them:
bright pink cheeks,
the globes that fill my eager palms
with their round wholeness,
palpable, improbably complete in morning
blowze of easy sun.
Their fragrance calms me.
Near them, all the world seems young,
so lovely,
light skin fuzzy on my tongue.

PARKING IN THE CONVERTIBLE AT NIGHT

We sat above the city,
slumped in seats beneath a billion stars
whose countless stories could be told.
The moon, too large, even tumescent,
beamed its idiotic light.

I beamed as well, so full of stories,
as you leaned toward me, listening
and fooled by sleights of hand,
forgetting that a billion stars were out there,
equally convincing, cool and vast.

HIGH SCHOOL

Everyone must go there.
None returns.

One sees the boys get into line,
their first mustache more like a wish
above their lips. The girls stand
parallel and pure, some of them bleeding,
all of them afraid. They've seen

their older sisters taken. They have seen
their older brothers, too,
assimilated, saturated, swept.

The hot brick building is a kind of furnace.
They're its fuel.

The hot brick building is a kind of maw
that feeds to frenzy.

Everyone must go there.
None returns.

FAMILY REUNION

So they arrive, the relatives again
in their tight shoes, the men with ties
as narrow as your finger,
shirts with shadows underneath the arms.
The women fill the doorframes with their hips.

They smell of fish, hot oil, and coffee.
One of them has wrung a chicken's neck
the night before and enters proudly
with her sloppy bag of broken wings
and breasts like hands folded in prayer.

The older women huddle in the den,
as round as ottomans,
these stumps of motherhood
without a pride of children at their feet.
They know the truth

about your uncle, who has not come in.
They know he lived as well as anyone
in that position could have lived,
given his lameness, deafness of an ear,
that turn of mind.

They just keep coming, even second cousins
twice removed. They're in your house
all day and night, spaghetti junction
of the roads you've traveled, more or less.
Their visit lasts, of course, forever.

MISJUDGMENTS

1.

The old crow, stumped as usual,
cannot believe
the shadow on the lawn is not his own.

2.

When the little swallows left their nest,
abandoning my porch for distant forests,
I was only happy.

Why am I so hesitant today?

THE IMPERIAL BED CHAMBER

The emperor's asleep in his big bed,
brocade of curtains hanging round his head.
You'd almost think that really he was dead.

The mouse must think so, nibbling on the cheese
between his toes. Lice lick his hair grease.
Busily, his crotch is full of fleas.

His kingdom reaches to the ends of earth,
but still he fits this teeming berth,
a feast for creatures who can taste his worth.

THE BIG PICTURE

You may have seen me, if you've seen the film.
I was among those waving from a window
as the big parade passed by below.
I stood there in another scene and listened
to the rousing speeches in the central square.
I was roused, of course.
When the tanks approached, you may
have seen men running in the distance
through the darkened city. I was there,
and running. The angle was unhelpful.
I was in the last frame of the picture,
with my name spelled wrong.
I do believe it's your name, too.
We were there, in History, somewhere.
On land, on sea, or in the air.

COVENANT IN APRIL

And so I make it with the ground itself,
which only deepens as I stand and dig,
this soil my home now, layer unto layer,
top and subsoil, crust and crumble.
Make it with the whole imagined earth
I catalogue by root and branch, by hand
and mouth, by what is said but mostly not.
With hard black coal that's hidden underneath,
immortal diamond-eye of truth.
With you, my star, that rises in the east
and takes a gaudy turn across the vault,
then settles into soft, alluvial terrain
in this wet month of pent-up buds,
when frivolous and fiery thoughts begin
and birds assemble, summoned from the south
like words almost forgotten but not quite.

CROW'S NEST

The moon has lost a sock in that dark meadow,
and the wind's gone south. I sit here
in the silver pre-dawn sky, all soot and shadow,
hoarfrost gathering between my toes. I know
that nothing's ever lost or gone: it's here
today and there again tomorrow. Snow
is rain is ripe corn, coal. The world can't show
itself at once. And so I'm sitting here,
I'm perched with patience, and can take it slow.

OLD TEAMS

Not one of them still walks among us,
who can stand and talk and bicker
and make love; they've lost their footing
in the world, gone under
pitch and pool, run off the tracks
where they once circled, golden-thighed
and sprightlier than crowds of lookers-on.
They're gone, the golfers in their wool plus-fours,
the divers in the suits with shoulder straps,
the quarterbacks in close-fit, leather helmets.

Looking in their eyes, behind the glass,
the glaze of decades, I can only wonder
what they make of me, this hovering
compassionate blank gaze from time beyond.
They would have to know
that I was coming, and that I would love them,
as I really do, for their blear innocence
and their fool faith in life to come.

THE BROKEN NECK

Her frosty-headed husband roughly snoring
never moved but grumbled in his sleep
as she went down to feed the cat at midnight,
pausing at the dizzy top of stairs,
then pitching forward, falling through the dark
into the cellar, headfirst, landing on her face.
A cold, clay floor whirling around her,
she lay dead awake, still, and could sense
the lost years waiting with a cap in hand,
her head above the clouds, a blur below.
Her limbs were children in a heavy sleep,
remote beside her as she lay there thinking
all too clearly, with the cat's white tail
and purring engine settled at her neck.

LEO

You were here before me, Leo:
father and my son.

I see your circle as it shines
through sunny haze—

a large unbroken circle
that encloses all my days.

I come and go, dear Leo,
in a world below

your arcing rainbow.
I am lost and won.

I walk this passage in-between.
I'm seen, unseen.

But you are luminous,
enormous, porous

and surrounding name.
Your single flame

warms both my hands,
my either side

on this cold passage
through an age

where everyone was born
before they died.

Not you, my Leo:
here before me and long after,

fiery constellation,
father and my son.

RISE

One thing happens, then another.
In the long slow rise, so many hands
reach out and lift us
over fallen branches, hidden drops,
old crops of stone. The moon
tilts up its yellow chin. The clouds
disperse. We grow into a face
our mothers recognize as someone else:
a father's father, sister's sister.
Nobody is single in this world,
that's all we know, will ever know,
about the way we come and go.
We're pulled to presence by a doctor's
urgent, gentle hands; we're laid
to sleep and covered over. Nobody's
alone. I'm here with you. Here
reaching for your fingers, holding on.

THE LIVING ROOMS OF SOUTH REBECCA

It's first the game shows,
then the talk shows,
then of course the movies until dawn.

You've seen them sitting
in the musty houses, in the fat
and fuzzy chairs, their blue feet up.

They're waiting for the last
good show on earth,
which certainly will come.

They rarely chat among themselves,
or visit other houses,
even switch the channel.

This is what they've come to,
old, infirm, or short of cards
to spread upon the table.

If they understand a little
less of each successive program,
this is not all bad.

THE TREES ARE GONE

Rebecca Avenue has lost its trees:
the willow that would brush against my window,
and the spruce that cooled our porch out back,
the ginko I would rake in mid-October,
with its matted leaves like Oriental fans.
Even the beech has been cut down,
that iron pillar of my mother's garden,
with its trunk so smooth against one's cheek.

The dirt I dug in has been spread
with blacktop: tar and oil. They've rolled it
blithely over sidewalk slate
where cracks once splintered into island tufts.
Even leafy hills beyond the town
have been developed, as they like to say:
those tinsel woods where I would rinse myself
in drizzle, in the pinwheel fall.

You can stand all day here without knowing
that it once knew trees: green over green
but gamely turning violet at dusk,
then black to blue-vermillion in the dawn.
It's sentimental, but I miss those trees.
I'd like to slip back through the decades
into deep, lush days and lose myself again
in leaves like hands, wet thrash of leaves.

WAITING ROOM

It has been some days since I came in,
or maybe months.
The tree outside the doctor's window
shuddered and became its blossoms;
later, it was green
with blood-bright clots of fruit in branches.
It unwound the colors of the world in time:
a crimson-orange, flame-vermilion.
Brown, then black,
its twiggy fingers reaching for the sky.
I've seen the girls becoming wives,
the boys dissolving into folds of skin.
I've monitored the periodic cries
behind closed doors and muffling walls.
The seats go empty
but the nurse retains a blithe demeanor
so I'm not afraid.
She's smiling now.
The doctor will be ready for me soon,
she says, so calm.
He's cleaning instruments
and putting sheets on his long table,
with that blinding eye-bulb on his head,
the lamp that fixes
with its lonely beam the next-in-line.

BEFORE A JOURNEY

After all-night rain in early fall,
the pavement glistens
and the grass is ankle-deep and wet.
The yellow birch has lost few leaves.

I stand beside the car
and lift my face into the cooling sun.
A slight wind burns my cheeks and chin.

The mountains, jade-green, fill the distance
with their vast, old stretch.

A wedge of geese moves slowly to the south.

I'm going far away as well.
But not today.

WHITE CANE

ETHEL AT THE HEARTH

Aunt Ethel could be found at night
beside the woodfire,
elbows out and working in the air
from which she drew her endless yarn,
the soft-spun texture
of a still-imaginary garment
growing in the spark-lit room before us
as she purled and plucked,
and we, the lucky ones, would lean
toward her with eyes and ears,
all ready to accommodate, inhabit
every sleeve and pocket,
twist and unexpected turn.

BORGES IN SCOTLAND

In the dismal garden at Pilmour
I watched old Borges, blind man leaning
on his stick among the iron trunks of beech,
a wind-dark canopy of claws above him.

Gusts of salt wind swayed the trees,
rippling the feathers of the bracken floor.
"It's rooks," he said, ears opening like palms.
The empty headlights of his eyes turned up.

So Borges listened and was birds.
A soot-cloud rose, world-blackening,
the hard-by thunder of a thousand birds
who called his name now: Borges, Borges.

AFTER THE BIG BANG

Hildegard of Bingen likened shadows
to the furrows left behind by ploughs,
to silence in the wake of well-said prayers.

Meaning follows from a certain burst,
the blunt initial blue-struck blade,
the bid for help, the consequential word.

A bang from nowhere, big or small,
can waken what was never seen before:
the fan-tailed planets, sizzling stars.

So once I asked you for a lift at dusk,
a cup of tea. I asked you for a hand,
a clasp, a kiss. I asked you for a life.

See that small shadow on the faint-lined page,
the word from nowhere like the world itself,
the godforsaken hand that holds this pen.

A flock of white gulls settles on the furrow,
frenzied over worms. I tilt the nib,
and everything that follows follows fast.

MIND

The wind knows nothing,
tossing every leaf and light blue hat
that it surrounds,
invisible but violent of purpose,
single-minded in its sweep
and unselective grasp of everything before.

The mind is like this,
moving forward, sideways, backwards
through the object-world,
undoing what was given, smothering,
unmaking in its wake, then making light
of its destruction, moving on.

A SHORT ADDRESS
TO THE ACADEMY OF SILENCE

*"After everything is said, the world will have
barely wakened to the noise."*
—Quintilian

It is not to speak but merely listen
that we come together: there are words enough
as wars enough and valentines enough.
The battlefields are littered with last notes
to far-off lovers, who will not be met;
they don't quite say whatever they had meant
to mean, the phrases failing under pressure.
It's often like that in the spoken world.
We must form academies of silence,
classes where the only sounds occur
when empty pages flutter in the gust
as tinny leaves rehearse their crumbling.

We have all been argued up and down;
been called, cajoled, corrected, and becalmed;
been left to memorize our p's and q's
and to march the words in serried numbers.
Free the vowels. They are just the wind,
and consonants are gates that swing on hinges.
Sacrifice the names, the times and dates:
those crude specifics history adores
and calls its own. We've surely had enough
of these: rebarbative articulations,
beeps, wild eeps, sosumi, quacks.
The sound-screen blank is best for now.

Let fall what falls and still befalls us,
but resist the urge to pin it down.
The goslings risen from the lake in flight
must not be sentenced to a noose of words,
however lovely. Soldiers never say
how hard they fell, how wet the blood was.
Lovers in the dawn don't need a garland
of good words to grant that it was good,
what happened in the dark. We rhetoricians
must attend the world as if in mourning
or profoundly awed by what is given.
We must say the least of it, and cease.

WHITE CANE

I've always guessed
at truth in shadows,
what lies low, beneath
the rippling pewter of the sea
or hard-packed dirt.
A blind man, tapping
as I go, without a vision
of the falling world.
But I've had access
through my nose, of course,
detecting rot.
I've felt the fungus
on the barks of trees,
heard coins *ka-ching*
in slot machines,
the slamming doors
and maddened dogs
and children asking (not
politely) for another bowl.
That taste of metal
on my tongue this morning:
what is that?
It won't be pretty
when at last I see,
but I have guessed so much
already, being such
a man of intuition, someone
who can move around the world,
a blind man, tapping.

POWER STATIONS

You'd think that, from a height, they'd disappear,
but astronauts report you still can see them
when so many other vivid features
disappear from view: these ganglia of wire,
rods and pistons, conical high towers
rising in a forest or on distant plains,
elaborately hidden from the common view.

A few of them, like Three Mile Island or Chernobyl,
call attention to themselves like teens
who suddenly must walk on some wild side.
They ruin everything around them, fail
at school, wind up in Rehab or the local jail.
Their reputations never will recover,
but their peers still hide and power on.

I came upon one in its monstrous glory
in the summer woods, leafing my way
through vast anthologies of heavy foliage.
For a brief while, standing in that vision,
I was all ablaze, part of its story.
Even now, far from that luminary site,
I feel the surge, the tingle, coming through.

THE LOST MANUSCRIPTS

Most of what I've written has been lost.
The house I lived in for so many years
burned to the ground, consuming pages
I had labored over for some decades.
I rewrote these things and liked the words
at least as much, with my revisions saying
more and sometimes less about what happened,
closer to the truth with every stroke.
My pen grew heavy, and my fingers cramped.
En route to that eternal city where
all night the fires of attention flare,
I lost the latest version of my work.
I left it on the platform, changing trains,
or underneath the seat of my blue carriage.
For a month or two, retracing steps,
I held out hope. This soon receded.
I returned to my old country place,
took out a notebook to begin again.
Perhaps it's better anyway like this,
with nothing to confirm my worst suspicions,
nothing to obstruct a sense that's breaking
even as I write, this blazing now.

NEAR OLD MELDRUM, AFTER A FUNERAL

—in memoriam Nick Bogdan

What a world, the godhead gone
but everywhere his bony little feet protruding,
blunt toes poking out from underneath
the blankets of the dawn,
the fields of rye.
His knobbly knees stick out through ledges,
and his tongue's a lacerating stream
through woods in early spring.
Those are his shoulders lifting hedges,
hips that bulge the downy heath.
His fingers climb the walls of sky.

BELIEF

I have one true life—
not seen, not heard
by anyone but me;
it penetrates, a knife
through buttery absurd,
invisible, a droneless bee
or razor wing of bird
passing through grief,
through heavy laughter,
word for word.

AFTER HOURS

I'm working in the dark and well past midnight,
fast awake,
with much at stake,
consumed by what comes easily and right
before the dawn,
with its blue shadows on the frosty lawn:
the work itself, its laughter and its tears,
this snake that eats its tail and disappears.

BY THE LIGHT OF MORNING SNOW

I shift from chair to chair uneasily
in my bright study, dipping into volumes
from the long white shelf
replete with half-remembered passages,
the lines I've followed through despair
of winter into early spring
so many times before.

                Outside,
the blunt, accumulating blank of snow
drapes grainy sheets
across the world's ten thousand objects:
finding (or refinding) elemental forms:
what once was made but somehow
in the desultory haze got lost, unfound.

Snow falling, fast, a near erasure
of the landscape memorized in volumes,
then discarded, left unread
till now, till now.

LARGE PROJECTS

The Great Wall had a purpose in its day.
How many hands it took, and even bribes,
to separate the Chinese wheat from chaff,
to keep apart the wild marauding tribes.

The pyramids as mighty tombs suggest
the pharoahs and their kin were hardly meek.
Beginning with a solid, widespread base,
the social classes narrowed to a peak.

In our high modern democratic states,
it takes a million man-hours to erect
a capitalist tower full of men
and women working at their little desks.

This morning in the yard, it startled me
to see how many ants moved in a line
en route to my back door. I wondered what
large project they, in marching, had in mind?

A LIFE SENTENCE

Beyond that woodlot and its lip of hill,
the brook's still talking.
                              Early winter,
and the snow's a soft-sift, dry-mouthed bluster.

Crows are blunt, monotonous objectors
to the live-long day, its rote performance
of the daily round, its iterations.

Winds say nothing but at such great length
that nobody around here gives a damn.

The pages of the field go blank again
beneath the snow.
                        I know I know
so little, it does not surprise me
there are kings and emperors and higher-ups
like FDR and JFK and LBJ.

Hierarchy helps us into meaning,
and I'm quite aware that parts of speech
cannot be given equal time,
that sentences adhere to given routes—
the rivering deep syntax of pure mind—
as subjects ply their way through verbs,
becoming predicates.
                          The brook runs on.
It empties somewhere, maybe far away.
It seeps through soil, a loamy silence,
dribbles into oceans without end.

ORIGIN OF A SPECIES

I came from nowhere anyone would know,
obscure beginnings in a cup of soup
the emperor was just about to drink.

He saw me and, for one brief shining moment,
looked intensely in my eyes,
then swallowed hard. The next thing

I remember vividly is water,
swimming in the hot swift yellow stream
of royal piss in his blue garden

on a moonlit night in ancient times.
Selective memory is hard at work here.
Maybe I was mangled in some turd.

However it all started, here I am:
Professor So-and-So, who came from nowhere
but is here today, before you, smiling.

HIDING IN PLAIN SIGHT

What's obvious, of course, cannot be known
or ever understood. It's on the lawn,

in full display, where nobody can see
its shape or color, how it looks like me

when I come close, or you when you draw near.
When terror strikes, it feels like fear.

When bright explosions pluck the night,
it turns gray shadows into black and white.

In darkness, it abides. The break of day
shatters its goblet with a crystal spray

so clear that nobody thinks otherwise.
It's here, like now, apparent to all eyes

that look, but through it. Right as rain
on rainy days; on sick days, pain.

It seeks its level, filling every glass
with what will pour, what comes to pass.

THE CRUCIFIXION

Woodmites burrowed through the beams,
delighting in the rot, the punky core.
A million ants marched up the hill,
lured by a honey-covered bun
dropped by a soldier, who could only dream
about the distant province where his mother
drew sweet water from the well
and where his father followed in the tracks
his father cut through sugar-loam of fields.
Pickpockets moved among the crowds
that dwindled to a few by afternoon;
they'd had more luck the day before,
when somebody whose crimes were better known
was hung to dry. Against the sky,
a dozen vultures wondered if the wind
would bear them up
through this long day and those that followed,
if the feast below was worth the wait.

THE HEAVEN TRAIN

This great train's going nowhere,
sitting in the railyard.
Rust grows round its wheels,
the lights inside the cars go dim.

There's baby Jesus, teething, on the lap
of some dull Mary,
who has not seen Joe in many months.

The twelve apostles in another car
are playing poker.
Peter is a cheat, and Luke
is washing down some yellow pills
with warm, flat beer.

As usual, it's Judas with the aces,
John who stares into the mist.
"Go get yourself a life," says Mark
to Matthew, who is all flushed out.

That's Paul there,
writing in the red caboose, and all alone:
so many letters he will never send.
He'll meet the engineer one day,
he's perfectly convinced.

Those pigeons on the roof
are fast asleep;
they look like doves to passengers
who gather on the narrow platform,
tickets in their hands,
their bags all packed and ready to ascend.

THE POPE ON THE SUBWAY

The Pope is making rounds today,
his pockets full of bread and tuna, cheapo wine.
He's dressed in sneakers, baggy pants.
You'd never really know he was the Pope.

It's come to this because the pomp
was long ago abandoned by the masses,
who prefer to sleep on Sunday mornings,
waking to the feast of their own bodies.

Often he has watched them, glass in hand,
French-kissing in the *strada*,
hustling sex and picking pockets;
few of them believe in what they're doing.

And so he goes, their only Pope,
disrobed, benevolent, and now inviting
children to the wobbly altar
of his bony knees, his warm embrace.

He breaks old bread and tunafish with men
who doze beneath the morning papers,
offers wine in tiny paper cups
to women on the lam.

This city isn't Rome, the cop explains.
You're not the Pope.
Get off the subway or I'll take you in.
What's with the crosses?

He can only smile and bless a man
who, like the rest of them,
cannot believe in grace abounding,
loaves and fishes, *vino* without end.

JUDAS IN HIS CUPS

It's always the Last Supper around here.
That's Him, of course, the long face lengthening
with evening shadows. He will go
His way to real destruction soon enough.
For now, it's "Which of you is loyal?
Who can spell my name frontwards and backwards?
Who believes me when I say the world
is this way, that?" If you complain,
He'll wash your feet. It's so...disarming.
How can you resist those big, sad eyes,
the way He mumbles when the king demands
a full account of everything He's done?
My god, the man can walk on water
and without pontoons. The girls go crazy
when he sings those hymns. The boys
begin to drool when he gets down beside them
in the muddy river, drowning all the lice
in their long hair, making them swoon.
I've seen the doves descending overhead,
their shit like pellets on the shiny water.
It is quite a spectacle, I'll give you that.
Oh Jesus, Jesus... He can race in rings
around a subject, ducking every question.
Loaves and fishes, pearls and swine: He makes
you crazy with the lines, the little stories
nobody can really understand. They coo,
they crumble at his feet. He must be smart,
if nobody can figure out the gist.

Way up there on the Mount, you should have seen them
running in tight circles, wagging tails.
The poor at heart jangled their pockets,
and the meek were basking in His glory.
I am not so overjoyed tonight.
I've had enough already of the sermons.
We have walked, a dozen of us, up and down
this Holy Land, three years or more
without a woman or a nice hot bath.
My feet are killing me. I'm almost broke.
And there He goes, raising that cup.
Drink this, remember me, I'll never leave you.
They all eat this up. I just don't get it.
Yadda, yadda, yadda. So it goes.
These suppers drag on through the night,
the candles and the wine, the whispered chants.
No wonder I can feel my temples throb.
I'm out of here today, maybe tomorrow.

APPLESEED

He's often here, our Johnny
on the fringe, a loose-knit spirit
in his motley shirt and tin pan hat,
his stick of hickory and bag of seeds.

He's going nowhere you or I would go.
He bows to ancient trees like elders,
moves among the weeds
with ease of kin.

You've seen him at the edge of town,
a wanderer, suspect, bent over
with a trowel, dazed, fruit-sweetened
as he gives and takes, then gives again.

The birds adore him, pecking
in his wake. Small children bounce
their pebbles from his hat. He smiles
and waves. He seems unfazed

when citizens object to his demands
for air and light, for rain
and tenderness. Without domain,
he shelters where he can.

No property he can't just carry
by himself. He's wary
of the church and all its creed.
His life's his deed.

The Indians among us meet him
at their campfires, listen
to his tales, accept his seeds.
They give him what he needs.

He's moving on, a wisp,
a wind that starts from nowhere
and that has no end. Our Johnny
on the fringe, our mad-mild Johnny.

LATE THOUGHTS

Impossible, the decades gone
with all the stars I've wished upon
still there. My wishing time is done.

From time to less of it, I leap
and learn a little what to keep
beside me. Down is always steep.

I fall. We all fall down at last,
turn every present into past
and wonder how it went so fast.

There's no one left but me and you,
it seems: a house, an empty shoe,
and nobody to say what's true

or false. Take what you need. No more.
Though no one's really keeping score.
Remember to pull shut the door.

THE ART OF SUBTRACTION

In the afternoon, in summer,
sitting by the pond, I did the math.
Subtraction was
the next best thing to insight I could manage.

Take away the house, the tree, the bird.
Get rid of walls, real or imagined.
Look for less in everything around you.

I became a snail with nothing but my shell
to carry forward. It was not
as bad as maybe you might think.

I pared the dictionary down as well,
saved only nouns like stones along a path,
saved verbs that moved in one direction.
Ancillary parts of speech
seemed pointless and could go to hell.

I'm back this afternoon, in autumn,
sitting where I used to,
trying, once again, to clear my head,
subtract the last things I don't need,
get down to only
what cannot be shaken loose or said.

OUTCROPS

Shouldering through soils
and grassy uplands,
they appear, obliquely
with a chipped blue gaze
and many-faceted
appealing faces

that would have us know
how everywhere
beneath the sand-crumbs,
under loam
and vegetable lushness
of the rising hill,

a massiveness inheres,
of which these glimpses
are the merest sign,
the mildest warning
of the world before us
and long after.

ROCK AND WATER

When all is said and done, undone,
it's rock and water.

When the salt and pepper has been passed,
the butter scooped.

When every prayer in every tongue
has long been uttered.

When the kiss turns cold,
the fondling gesture frozen tight.

When war and peace, *folie à deux*,
have found each other

wanting and gone home, at last, for good,
it's rock and water.

from ANTHRACITE COUNTRY
(1982)

BEGINNING THE WORLD

The crossing from sleep to waking
was easy those early winter mornings
when the snow fell dumb and bright as stars.

My mother packed me to the nose
in scarves; she tied a hat to my head
and sent me stumbling in boots through hills of snow.

The way was a desert of white;
dunes whirling in the street where cars
lay buried: humped and sleeping camels.

And I loved that whiteness,
the unyielding blankness of it all
that left me alone with the whole world unimagined.

Today, marooned by decades
and distance from those days and winters,
I close my eyes to begin the world again.

WALKING THE TRESTLE

They are all behind you, grinning,
with their eyes like dollars, their shouts
of *dare you, dare you, dare you*
broken by the wind. You squint ahead
where the rusty trestle wavers into sky
like a pirate's plank. And sun shines
darkly on the Susquehanna, forty feet
below. You stretch your arms
to the sides of space and walk
like a groom down that bare aisle.
Out in the middle, you turn to wave
and see their faces breaking like bubbles,
the waves beneath you flashing coins,
and all around you, chittering cables,
birds, and the bright air clapping.

PLAYING IN THE MINES

Never go down there, fathers told you,
over and over. The hexing cross
nailed onto the door read DANGER, DANGER.
But playing in the mines once every summer,
you ignored the warnings. The door
swung easier than you wished; the sunlight
followed you down the shaft a decent way.
No one behind you, not looking back,
you followed the sooty smell of coal dust,
close damp walls with a thousand facets,
the vaulted ceiling with a crust of bats,
till the tunnel narrowed, and you came
to a point where the playing stopped.
You heard old voices pleading in the rocks;
they were all your fathers, longing to fix you
under their gaze and to go back with you.
But you said to them NEVER, NEVER,
as a chilly bile washed round your ankles.
You stood there wailing your own black fear.

THE MISSIONARY VISITS
OUR CHURCH IN SCRANTON

He came to us every other summer
from the jungles of Brazil,
his gabardine suit gone shiny in the knees
from so much praying.

He came on the hottest Sunday, mid-July,
holding up a spear before our eyes,
the very instrument, we were told,
which impaled a brace of his Baptist colleagues.

The congregation wheezed in unison,
waiting for the slides: the savage women
dandling their breasts on tawny knees,
the men with painted buttocks
dancing in a ring.

The congregation loosened their collars,
mopped their brows, all praying
that the Lord would intervene.

Always, at the end, one saw the chapel:
its white-baked walls, the circle of women
in makeshift bras, the men in shirts.

They were said to be singing a song of Zion.
They were said to be wishing us well in Scranton.

THE MINER'S WAKE
—in memoriam E. P.

The small ones squirmed in suits and dresses,
wrapped their rosaries round the chair legs,
tapped the walls with squeaky shoes.

But their widowed mother, at thirty-four,
had mastered every pose of mourning,
plodding the sadness like an ox through mud.

Her mind ran well ahead of her heart,
making calculations of the years without him
that stretched before her like a humid summer.

The walnut coffin honeyed in sunlight;
calla lilies bloomed over silk and satin.
Nuns cried heaven into their hands,

while I, a nephew with my lesser grief,
sat by a window, watching pigeons
settle onto slag like summer snow.

COAL TRAIN

Three times a night it woke you
in middle summer, the Erie Lackawanna,
running to the north on thin, loud rails.
You could feel it coming a long way off:
at first, a tremble in your belly,
a wire trilling in your veins, then diesel
rising to a froth beneath your skin.
You could see the cowcatcher,
wide as a mouth and eating ties,
the headlight blowing a dust of flies.
There was no way to stop it.
You lay there, fastened to the tracks
and waiting, breathing like a bull,
your fingers lit at the tips like matches.
You waited for the thunder of wheel and bone,
the axles sparking, fire in your spine.
Each passing was a kind of death,
the whistle dwindling to a ghost in air,
the engine losing itself in trees.
In a while, your heart was the loudest thing,
your bed was a pool of night.

SNAKE HILL

The dirt road rose abruptly through a wood
just west of Scranton, strewn by rusty wire,
abandoned chassis, bottles, bits of food.

We used to go there with our girls, those nights
in summer when the air like cellophane
stuck to your skin, scaling the frenzied heights

of teenage lust. The pebbles broke like sparks
beneath our tires; we raised an oily dust.
The headlights flickered skunk-eyes in the dark.

That way along the hill's illuminated crown
was Jacob's ladder into heaven; cars
of lovers, angel-bright, drove up and down.

There was a quarry at the top, one strip
worked out, its cold jaws open, empty-mouthed.
A dozen cars could park there, hip to hip.

There I took Sally Jarvis, though we sat
for six hours talking politics. I was
Republican, and she was Democrat.

We talked our way through passion, holding hands:
the moon, gone egg-yolk yellow in the sky,
tugged firmly at our adolescent glands.

I kissed her once or twice, far too polite
to make a rude suggestion, while the stars
burned separately, hard as anthracite.

The city was a distant, pinkish yawn
behind our backs as we leant head to head.
The dead-end quarry held us there till dawn.

THE LACKAWANNA AT DUSK

Here is a river lost to nature,
running in its dead canal
across the county, scumming its banks.
I lean out over the water,
poking my head through rusty lace
of the old rail bridge and blowing
my spits out into the swill.
A slow wind ushers the homely smell
around my head; I breathe its fumes.
In whirlpool eddies, odds
of garbage and poisoned fish
inherit the last red hour of light.
A ripe moon cobbles the waters.
Mounds of culm burn softly into night.

ANTHRACITE COUNTRY

The culm dump burns all night,
unnaturally blue, and well below heaven.
It smolders like moments almost forgotten,
the time when you said what you meant
too plainly and ruined your chance of love.

Refusing to dwindle, fed from within
like men rejected for nothing specific,
it lingers at the edge of town, unwatched
by anyone living near. The smell now
passes for nature. It would be missed.

Rich earth-wound, glimmering
rubble of an age when men
dug marrow from the land's dark spine,
it resists all healing.
Its luminous hump cries comfortable pain.

LEARNING TO SWIM

That summer in Tunkhannuk the cold stream
barked, dogs herding over stones. Behind me,
wading with a switch of willow in your hand,
you drove me out: large father
with your balding, sun-ripe head, quicksilver

smiles. I wavered over pebbles,
small, white curds, and listened into fear:
the falls that sheared the stream close by,
the gargle and the basalt boom.
"It's safe," you said. "Now go ahead and swim."

I let it go, dry-throated, lunging.
Currents swaddled me from every side,
my vision reeling through the upturned sky.
Half dazed and flailing in a whelm of cries,
I felt your big hand father me ashore.

THE SEA LILY

I found it on a culm bank near Old Forge:
the fossil of an ancient crawler
printed firmly in a slab of coal.
I took it home, the image if its delicate
horned shell and pincer-claws.

That summer in my bedroom, late one night,
I woke: a green moon eerily aflame
had caught the fossil in its funnel-light.
The creature shone, its eyes
were globed fruit swaying on their stems.

Last night I saw it shining in a dream,
the cilia on fire. Unnerved, I fossicked
in a book to find its name,
a miner in the word-bank, digger
in the tongue's lost gleaming quarry.

AMORES (AFTER OVID)

An afternoon in sultry summer.
After swimming, I slept on the long divan,
dreaming of a tall brown girl.

Nearby, a din of waves
blasted in the jaws of rocks.
The green sea wrestled with itself
like a muscular beast in the white sun.

A tinkle of glasses woke me: Corinna!
She entered with fruit and wine.
I remember the motion of her hair
like seaweed across her shoulders.

Her dress: a green garment.
She wore it after swimming.
It pressed to the hollows of her body
and was beautiful as skin.

I tugged at the fringe, politely.
She poured out wine to drink.
"She thing," I whispered.

She held the silence with her breath,
her eyes to the floor, pretending
then smiling: a self-betrayal.

In a moment she was naked.
I pulled her down beside me,
lively, shaking like an eel—
loose-limbed and slippery-skinned.
She wriggled in my arms at play.

When I kissed her closer
she was wet beneath me and wide as the sea.

I could think of nothing but the sun,
how it warmed my spine as
I hugged her, shuddering all white light,
white thighs. Need more be said
but that we slept as if
the world had died together with that day?

These afternoons are rare.

SWIMMING IN LATE SEPTEMBER

We listen:
the hush of apples falling through a dark,
the crackling of pines.
A slow wind circles the pond
like an ancient bird with leathery wings.

I float, my belly to the moon,
lifting my toes through cold, black water.
You brush against me, fanning your hair,
so close we are touching head to foot.

Frog-eyes sparkle in the ferns
as if they wonder
who would be swimming in late September.
Already the crickets have lost their wings;
the woods are brittle yellow.

But we go on swimming, swimming.
It is part of our love.
We give off rings of chilly waves
from one still center. Tonight
there is nothing but skin between us:
the rest is water.

TO HIS DEAR FRIEND, BONES

The argument against restraint
in love, in retrospect, seems quaint;
I would have thought this obvious
to you, at least, whose serious
pursuit of intellectual grace
is not less equal to your taste
for all things richly formed. No good
will come of what we force. I should
be hesitant to say how long
this shy devotion has gone on,
how days beyond account have turned
to seasons as we've slowly learned
to speak a common tongue, to find
the world's erratic text defined
and stabilized. I should be vexed
to mention time at all, except
that, even as I write, a blear
October dampness feels like fear
externalized; I number days
in lots of thirty— all the ways
we have for counting breaths, so brief,
beside the measures of our grief
and joy. So let me obviate
this cold chronology and state
more simply what I mean: it's sure
enough, the grave will make obscure
whatever fierce, light moments love
affords. I should not have to prove
by metaphysical displays
of wit how numerous are the ways
in which it matters that we touch,
not merely with out hearts; so much
depends upon the skin, dear bones,
with all its various, humid tones,
the only barrier which contrives
to keep us in our separate lives.

THIS REAPING

They are all going out around us,
popping off like lights—
the professors crumpled over desks,
the doctors with entrails hanging from their ears,
the operators dead at the end of lines.

They are all going out, shut off
at the source without warning—
the student tumbled from a bike in traffic,
the child in its cradle, choking,
the nun in a faulty subway.

Any nobody know the hour,
whether now or later, whether
neatly with a snap in the night
or, less discreetly, dragged
by a bus through busy corners.

What a business, this reaping
in private or public places
with so little sowing:
let us pray that somewhere
on sweaty beds of complete affection
there are lovers
doubling themselves in the lively dark.

SKATER IN BLUE

The lid broke, and suddenly the child
in all her innocence was underneath
the ice in zero water, growing wild
with numbness and with fear. The child fell
so gently through the ice that none could tell
at first that she was gone. They skated on
without the backward looks that might have saved
her when she slipped, feet first, beneath the glaze.
She saw the sun distorted by the haze
of river ice, a splay of light, a lost
imperfect kingdom. Fallen out of sight,
she found a blue and simple, solid night.
It never came to her that no one knew
how far from them she'd fallen or how blue
her world had grown so quickly, at such cost.

SUMMER PEOPLE

See them, the affectionate ones,
how they dawdle in the sun on watered lawns,
how they cast one shadow and call it love.

See the husbands playing at tennis,
shouting the scores, their smooth limbs
perfect in all proportions,

bobbing and weaving, winning or losing
weight and wives. Some knees are
bandaged to support their passion.

It is so important, they say,
knowing how to serve, not balking
when you swing, staying close to the line.

See the slender ladies with children
who look like themselves; they have married
these men with long vacations,

these summery people who know how
to do it, year after year,
how to find the time, the beautiful

houses on winking lakes, the friends
with even more luck than themselves,
the words to endear them each to another.

BLACK WEEK

I must parse the sentence of my sadness,
diagram despair.
I must break my anger into parts of speech:
the nouns of nothing I can do or say,
the verbs of ruin, participles
raging through my fevered nights.
I must find a stronger subject for my verbs,
disrupt the syntax of protracted fear.
I must place my anger in subordination,
possess the grammar of my own recovery,
find my predicate, someone gladly
to complete my transitive, hungry verbs.

NEAR ABERDEEN

"History broods over that part of the world like the easterly haar.
—R.L. Stevenson

On a blue scarp, far out, musing
over water, standing where the salt winds
whet their blades on granite edges,
hogweeds rasping, marram grass and thistle,
I was north of Aberdeen,
alone and calling to a friend
as if the wind could carry to her heart
my words like spores, as if
by merely shouting in the air
past waters snarling in the rocks,
affection could be raised, its sword
and fire, the blue flame
rising in the mist, the lifting haar.

from TOWN LIFE
(1988)

THE VISITORS

Our children sleep among the stars:
blunt, bodiless, unnamed.
The music of their sphere is one long vowel.
None has been signaled from the ground by us,
at least not yet.
Mere argument will never bring them down,
since accidental entry is their mode,
a rupture into flesh,
the starlight overhead past recollection.
Their going will be difficult as well:
a disremembering, consonants disowed.
That change will hurt like every other change.
Only in the spring,
when new grass skims a sudden world,
will any of them understand our need,
our wishing we could hold them,
say their names and set them down.

DIFFERENTIATION

Already the brow begins to knit,
the arm-buds reach for freedom from the mass,
the eyeholes deepen.

Delicate, the spine uncurls and lengthens,
ganglia and nerves by slow degrees
inhabit what we used to call the soul.

A small pulse separates on its own time,
and none of this is me,
or you, or us.

Brainwaves scatter in the blank of night,
a splay of light from
some new star.

And gently in the amniotic drowse
its face begins to shine,
a lucent stare.

Soon every feature will believe its name,
and tight fists beat across
the broken water.

CROPS

And there is sadness in the way they grow—
bell peppers at full gong in mid-July,
the corn breast-high
where mudprints followed me uphill in May,
loud snapping fingers, peas or beans,
the feathery and light-engorging dill,
the long-haired chives or rough-tongued mint,
engaging basil,
my fair son,
his tendril body climbing through the air.

HISTORY

History has many corridors, yes,
and floodlit stages where the folks
with greater parts than we have
romp, cavort, and trade bold gestures
that affect us all,
and sooty alleys where you'd only go
for love or money;
it's a steeply winding stair,
a sliding board, a tunnel or a ramp,
depending on your gravity of mind
or point of view— but all
the same, the level years
like floors that tumble through a burning house
and come to rest, blue cinders,
on the ground where all things subject
to the laws of change must come to rest,
the shelf of now,
this moment over breakfast
as we touch warm fingers over
toast and jam
and say, okay, I'm glad you're here,
no matter what we said or did before,
I'm glad you're here.

IN THE SPHERE OF COMMON DUTY

Telemachus did well, I think, to stay,
in spite of what his father might have said
about the promise written in the stars.
The island was all right, nothing fantastic,
but he called it home, then made it home
by taking on himself the fond discharge
of homely duties—taking out the trash,
deciding which of nature's green-leaved things
one should call "weeds" and separate to mulch,
accepting that it's infinitely harder
to stay put than rush away. Ulysses would have
loved the grand illusion that adventures hang
on precipices, passions, clashing rocks:
the crude near-misses of the manly life;
he went off to war, as men still do,
for reasons the community allowed
were just and not just his. But once the Trojans
had been done to death: What then? What then?
"Boys will be boys," they always say.
Think of him, Telemachus, who loved the stars
no less for watching them from where he stood.

READING THROUGH THE NIGHT

Late reading, and our books dissolve
in thunder, lightning through the rain;
their lights burn single in the mind.

Your novel and my novel move together,
line by line, like Noah's animals,
who found the ark, each other as the flood-

tide rose. Our oaky bed, its headboard
of a prow, lifts over waves. Your hero
and my heroine engage, as night whelms over

and the one great plot, that salty stew,
as ever, thickens. In a single sheet, we feel
the rise and fall of breath, the generations

that have come and gone and come again.
Is nothing ever lost? Eternal climax,
denouement: we find ourselves, at dawn,

on that bare hillside, disembarked,
the animals afoot, our novels turning
on themselves again, their separate spines.

THE FUNCTION OF WINTER

I'm for it, as the last leaves shred
or powder on the floor, as sparrows find
the driest footing, and November rains
fall hard as salt sprayed over roads.
The circulating spores take cover
where they can, and light runs level
to the ground again; no more the vertical
blond summer sheen that occupies a day,
but winter flatness—light as part of things,
not things themselves. My heart's in storage
for the six-month siege we're in for here,
laid up for use a little at a time
like hardtack on a polar expedition,
coveted though stale. Ideas, which in
summer hung a crazy jungle in my head,
subside now, separate and gleam in parts;
I braid them for display on winter walls
like garlic tails or onions, crisp bay wreaths.
One by one, I'll pluck them into spring.
If truth be told, I find it easier
to live this way: the fructifying boom
of summer over, wild birds gone, and wind
along the ground where cuffs can feel it.
Everything's in reach or neatly labeled
on my basement shelves. I'm ready to begin
to see what happened when my heart was hot,
my head too dazzled by itself to think.

SUBURBAN SWAMP

The swamp at the end of our cozy country road
does nothing for the value of what we own.
It's what the agents call an eyesore
and the neighbors never mention to their friends,
half wishing what they never set in words
will not exist. I'm standing by the stumps
that fizzle like antacid tabs in water,
the tatty oaks too old for leaves, loose
at the roots like blackened teeth that wobble
in the gums, a periodontal nightmare.
This was once a lake, old-timers say,
remembering the sunny Sunday picnics
where these mossbanks grow or, some say,
"fester." Frogs exhale into the midday air.
The green-gold water pops its blisters.
Winds are redolent of larval scum
that might well be a soothing balm for backache
in an old wives' tale if old wives lived.
The Indians came out in bark canoes
two centuries ago; now Boy Scouts tramp
the margins for a merit badge or two,
birdwatchers wait for oddly feathered friends,
and secret moralists inspect the setting
for its sheer decay. I like it how
what happens happens out of sight here.
Business goes on beneath the surface:
transformations: water into froth,
great hulking logs to pulp and steam.
Here every change is hidden but complete,
all purposes obscured— a skilled dismantling,
de-creation into light and air.

PASSING THROUGH VERMONT ON THREE MARTINIS

For purple miles the mountains rise
above the river. Barns
assemble in surrounding corn.
The traveler takes nothing here for granted,
tippling under ice-and-vodka skies.
He listens to the water's racy babble
and discerns a meaning. Even
when the wind yanks back a shutter,
he perceives a sign. A farm boy
fishing in the distance moves him
more than a museum. Cowbells
tinkle in the distant calm.
He vows to quit his salaried position
one fine day, returning to this spot
to sip forever as the mountains rise.

THIS KAMPUCHEA

We sit in a *tuk-tuk* with binoculars,
sipping Fantas, as a hot white wind
blows over water half a mile wide—
a heat that most of us can just abide.
Pale tourists, young voyeurs: we find
humidity a subject. Kids with scars

across their cheeks and narrow backs beg
candies, cigarettes. We give them coins
that mean so little we can hardly not afford
to give them up. Such charity! I pour
my Fanta in a cup and give a swig
to a small boy whose mother joins

us from behind a shack, an improvised
bamboo construction housing refugees.
She hasn't said a word since she escaped,
the doctor tell us. Maybe she was raped
at knifepoint, maybe she had seen the trees
strung out with villagers Pol Pot despised

for simply being there. Then we all hear
they shot her husband in a ditch before her eyes;
her eyes seem blank now, darkly blank.
I notice that she never seems to blink
but watches like the bald-eyed moon, in fear,
as children utter their unlovely cries

for candy, cigarettes, for sips of Fanta
from my tinny cup. The bamboo clicks
in big-finned leaves across the river where
Cambodia has turned in its despair
to Kampuchea, where the golden bricks
of Angkor Wat sink like Atlantis

into jungle depths, the lost bright heart
of ancient quietude that's since been drowned
in spit and blood. I wonder why we came
to this sad border and if we're to blame
as much as anyone in that swart
jungle where the millions died as Death found

easy entrance to the world, engorged
itself, while faces turned another way.
Lon Nol, Pol Pot, the bloated Princes
whom the Rouge detested: none convinces
us that he's to blame. We'll never say
"this one" or "that" and feel relieved, purged

and guiltless, free to sail by 747
home to seasons in the hills of ease.
This Kampuchea has become a tomb
inside me, alien, but still a home
in some strange way—an altar where my knees
will fall at intervals, an odd chance given

to me as a gift, a place to bow
in obeisance to the darkest gods
who rule the heart whenever we ignore
our greatest charge: to watch and pray. The shore-
line glistens as a boy lets down a bamboo
rod, an old man settles by a tree and nods

off into dreams, a flame-bright bird
sails over water without any sense
of human borders. Children scurry to a jeep
beside us where the spoils are greater, as we keep
to schedule and drive away: untold expense
now memorized as what we saw and heard.

GRANDMOTHER IN HEAVEN

In a plume-field, white above the blue,
she's pulling up a hoard of rootcrops
planted in a former life and left to ripen:
soft gold carrots, beets, bright gourds.
There's coffee in the wind, tobacco smoke
and garlic, olive oil and lemon.
Fires burn coolly through the day,
the water boils at zero heat.
It's always almost time for Sunday dinner,
with the boys all home: dark Nello,
who became his cancer and refused to breathe;
her little Gino, who went down the mines
and whom they had to dig all week to find;
that willow, Tony, who became so thin
he blew away; then Julius and Leo,
who survived the others by their wits alone
but found no reason, after all was said,
for hanging on. They'll take their places
in the sun today at her high table,
as the antique beams light up the plates,
the faces that have lately come to shine.

AT THE RUINED MONASTERY IN AMALFI
—*for Charles Wright*

On a hill, approaching Easter,
well above the sea's bland repetitions
of the same old story
and the town's impenitent composure,
I survey old grounds.

The fire-winged gulls engulf the tower.
Lesser grackles, nuns and tourists,
scatter on the grass.

The brandy-colored light of afternoon
seeps through the stonework;
creeping flowers buzz and flutter
in the limestone cracks.

Wisteria-choked loggias drip with sun.

A honeycomb of cells absorbs the absence
it has learned to savor;
court and cloister close on silence,
the auroral prayers long since burned off
like morning fog.

The business of eternity goes on behind our backs.

In the chapel dark,
I'm trying to make out a worn inscription
on a wind-smudged altar,
but the Latin hieroglyphs have lost their edge.

Remember me, *Signore*,
who has not yet learned to read your hand,
its alphabet of buzz and drip and flutter.

from HOUSE OF DAYS
(1998)

STARS FALLING

Fire-flakes, flints: the same old stars
still fiery in the unredemptive sky,
the silvery and hopeless midnight sky
that feels like home from here to Mars,
then gradually grows foreign into stars
we hardly recognize, that fill the eye
with lofty gleanings we ineptly scry
by framing legends of unending wars.

There is some comfort in the way they sprawl,
their vast composure in the cold and careless
spaces that absorb them as they fall,
their dwindling into dark with less and less
of anything a witness might recall,
the ease of their becoming homelessness.

SWIMMING AFTER THOUGHTS
—in memoriam Robert Penn Warren

Across the blackened pond and back again,
he's swimming in an ether all his own;

lap after lap, he finds the groove
no champion of motion would approve,

since time and distance hardly cross his mind
except as something someone else might find

of interest. He swims and turns, inching
his way through frogspawn, lily pads, and shaking

reeds, a slow and lofty lolling stroke
that cunningly preserves what's left to stoke

his engines further, like a steamwheel plunging
through its loop of light. He knows that lunging

only breaks the arc of his full reach.
He pulls the long, slow oar of speech,

addressing camber-backed and copper fish;
the minnows darken like ungathered wishes,

flash and fade— ideas in a haze of hopes
ungathered into syntax, sounding tropes.

The waterbugs pluck circles round his ears
while, overhead, a black hawk veers

to reappraise his slithering neck, and frogs
take sides on what or who he is: a log

or lanky, milk-white beast. He goes on swimming,
trolling in the green-dark glistening

silence and subtending mud where things
begin, where thoughts amass in broken rings

and surface, break to light, the brokered sound
of lost beginnings: fished for, found.

RAIN BEFORE NIGHTFALL

Late August, and the long soft hills
are wet with light:
a silken dust, with shifting thunder
in the middle distance. Chills
of fall have not yet quite
brought everything to ruin.
And I stop to look, to listen
under eaves. The yellow rain
slides down the lawn,
it feathers through the pine,
makes lilacs glisten,
all the waxy leaves. The air
is almost fit for drinking,
and my heart is drenched,
my thirst for something
more than I can see
is briefly quenched.

THE LAKE HOUSE IN AUTUMN

There's silence in the house at summer's wake.
The last leaves fall in one night's wind,
the mice are eaten, and the cats begin
a rumbling sleep. There's nothing much at stake.
It's not quite cold enough to stoke
the furnace, and the neighbors never seem to mind
if leaves are raked. I'm staring through a blind
at less and less beside a cooling lake.

I keep forgetting that this absence, too,
must be imagined. What is still unknown
is still beyond me, as with you.
The mind is darker, deeper than a windblown
lake that tries to mirror every hue
of feeling as the season takes me down.

A KILLING FROST

Beside the pond in late November,
I'm alone again
as apples drop in chilly woods
and crows pull tendons like new rubber
from a roadkill mass.

Ice begins to knit along the ground,
a bandage on the summer's wounds.
I touch the plait
of straw and leafmold, lingering to smell
the sweet cold crust.

An early moon is lost
in sheer reflection,
wandering, aloof and thinly clad,
its eye a squint of expectation.

I know that way,
this looking for a place to land
where nothing gives,
these boundaries of frost and bone.

THE LOST SCENT

Winds off the dumps bring back a childhood
gone, long gone:
the reek of acid-tinged mine water,
smolder of the culm in lowly humps
beside the graveyard
where my father's father's drift in seams.

I've tried to lose so many things,
too many things,
and now this wind refuses to die down;
it carries in its multiple, gray folds
these whiffs and gleanings
from another life, once all my own.

TO MY FATHER IN LATE SEPTEMBER

A cold sky presses at my window,
and the leaves at every edge go brown.
I watch and listen,
though the walls are thick between us now.
The apples on the tree inside the garden
fall, unpicked. I let them fall
as I must fall and you, my father,
too must fall and sooner
than I'm willing yet to grant.
These blunt successions still appall me:
father into son to dying son,
the crude afflictions of a turning world
that still knows nothing and will never
feel a thing itself, this rock
that's drilled and blasted, cultivated,
left to dry or burn. We soon must learn
its facelessness in sorrow,
learn to touch and turn away,
to settle in the walls of our composure
and assume a kind of winter knowledge,
wise beyond mere generation
or the ruthless overkill of spring.

1954

Warm rain in winter,
and for days the streets
were all awash
in downtown Scranton,
gray snow melting,
sewers overwhelmed.
I went to school without
a hat, without
a thought of what
might follow: flood
or fright, unnatural
disasters. Hours
into dusk I drummed
my fingers on the desk
at school as windows
darkened and the glass
was streaked. My teacher
wept, I don't know why.
I found my mother crying
in the kitchen. I do not
know why. Sometimes
the waters must give way,
the skies tear open,
barrels overflow
and gutters run.

THE CROW-MOTHER TELLS ALL

The empty oil drums rattled in the yard
that day in Scranton, and the ham-red hills
would shudder in the distance, thunder-chilled.
My mother shucked a dozen ears of corn,
feeding me stories of the swoop and killings
I could say by heart and still can say.
She hovered in the dust-light, railed
as porch lamps flickered and the power failed,
but not in her. The boom-and-tingle of the storm
was half by her imagined. Hanging on the hard
wings of her apron, always in her sway,
I listened as the green ears all were torn,
her face by lightening cracked and clawed,
her laughter tumbling, beaked and cawed.

A CONVERSATION IN OXFORD
—*in memoriam Isaiah Berlin*

Euphonious if not in sync the bells
beat time in amber chapel towers,
and the time has come for tea and talk.
We settle in a room of many shades,
the questions you have spent the decades turning.

"What can we assume about this world?"
you wonder, once again. "What can we claim?"
So little, it would seem. The weak foundations
of all human knowledge make one shudder
to assume too much, to claim too boldly,

"What do you believe?" you ask, so frankly
that I redden, turn, avert my eyes.
"Is consciousness itself an end or foretaste
of a fuller life? This 'oversoul' that Emerson
proposed: Whatever does it mean?"

The honeying facades along the High Street
seem impervious to dwindling light,
whole generations are absorbed
in rheumy passages and darkened cloisters
where so many questions have been put

and left unanswered. It was not a failure
not to answer. I assume that you,
over the decades, have refused to grant
those easy answers that can dull a heart,
occlude a mind, can chain a soul.

You tap your pipe and offer this:
"Real liberty is found in gradations,
dartings of the mind —not Big Ideas—
which are mostly preludes to deceit,
embodiments of someone's will-to-power."

I scan the rows of volumes you have filled
with annotations in the well-kept nights—
from Plato to Descartes, from Kant to Kripke.
Herzen was a friend, and Vico, too.
You say that all the best books seize us

half by chance, interrogate and turn us
loose upon ourselves again. I mostly listen,
letting what you say fill up the hour.
The room grows violet and dusky,
insubstantial, as your voice compels

and seems to quicken as your flesh dissolves.
And soon the darkness is itself complete,
consuming everything except your language,
which assumes an Old World gaiety and calm.
I feel, myself, an apparition.

"It is strange," I say. "We find ourselves
alive without a reason, inarticulate
but always trying to re-form a thought
in words that never seem quite right."
I see a flicker in your candle-eyes.

"The world is what it is," you answer strictly,
having seen enough of it to say.
"The world is what you claim it is
as well: this dwindling light, the smoke
of reason, ghostly words in ghostly air."

So I claim this hour, a plum-deep dusk,
the need to pose so many questions,
late, so late— an Oxford afternoon
when everything but language falls away
and words seem all the world we need.

NEAR PITLOCHRY

As the sun cut through a cloud,
the hills lit up
like bulbs switched on by unseen hands;
the wind began its spiral climb
from hutch to valley
to the saw-toothed crags where thistle burns.
Alone, in winter,
with my face toward a frost-lit bush,
I waited and was met.

I WAS THERE

I say it, I was there.
No matter what the yellow wind has taken,
I was there, with you.
We have walked out early in the spring
beside the river, when the sun's red shield
was caught in branches
and the bud-tips bled.
We have plucked ripe berries from a hill of brush
in mid-July,
and watched the days go down in flames
in late September,
when the poplar shook its foil.
We have walked on snow in January light:
the long white fields were adamantly bright.
I say it, I was there.
No matter that the evidence is gone,
we heard the honking of the long black geese
and saw them float beyond the town.
Gone all those birds, loose-wristed leaves,
the snowfire, days
we cupped like water in our hands.
So much has slipped through fragile hands.
The evidence is lost, but not these words.
You have my word:
I say it, I was there.

Jay Parini was born in 1948 in Pittston, Pennsylvania. He was educated at Lafayette College and the University of St. Andrews in Scotland. In addition to four previous volumes of poetry, he has published six novels, two books of criticism, and biographies of John Steinbeck, Robert Frost, and William Faulkner. He has won several awards and fellowships, including a Guggenheim, the *Chicago Tribune* Heartland Award, and the Hale Medal for Literature. He teaches at Middlebury College in Vermont, where he lives with his wife, Devon Jersild, and their three sons.